Whale Watch

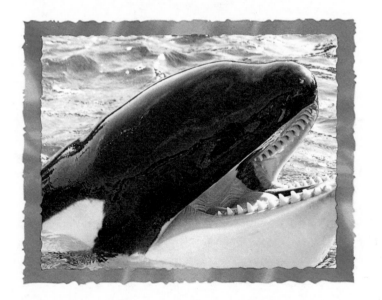

Written by Judy Spevack

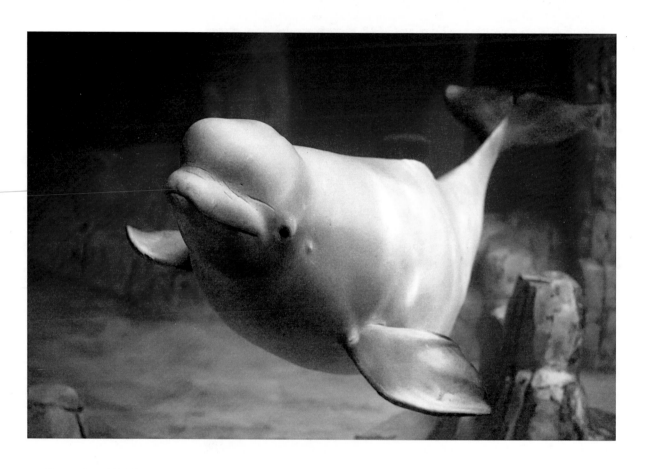

2

We watch white whales.

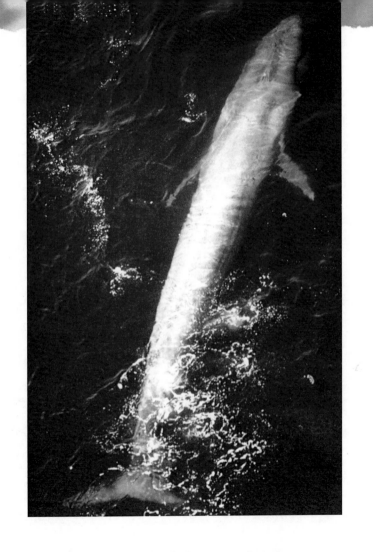

We watch blue whales.

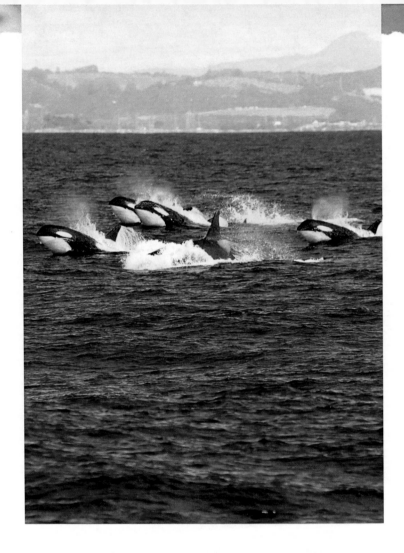

We watch black whales.

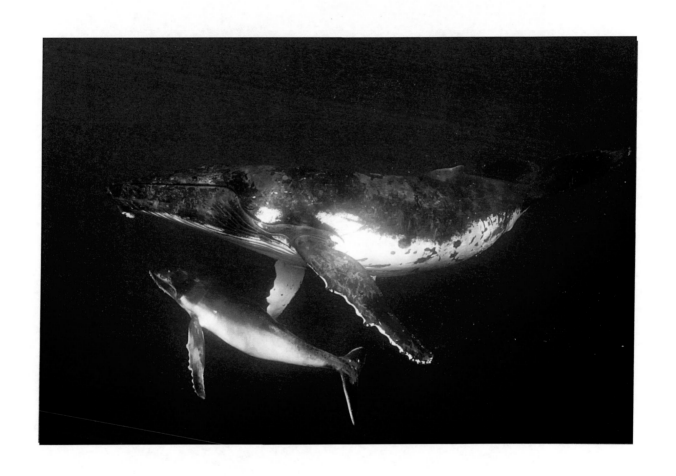

We watch new whales.

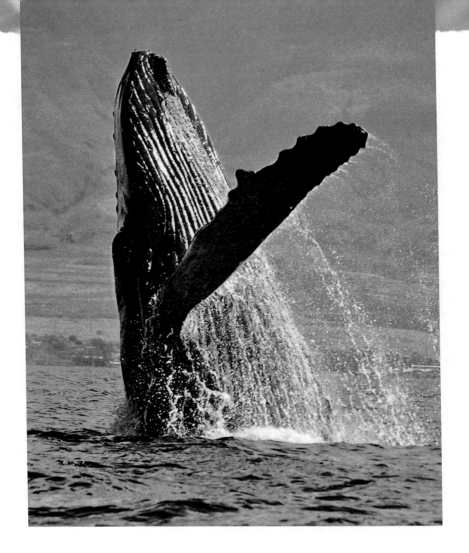

We watch one whale.

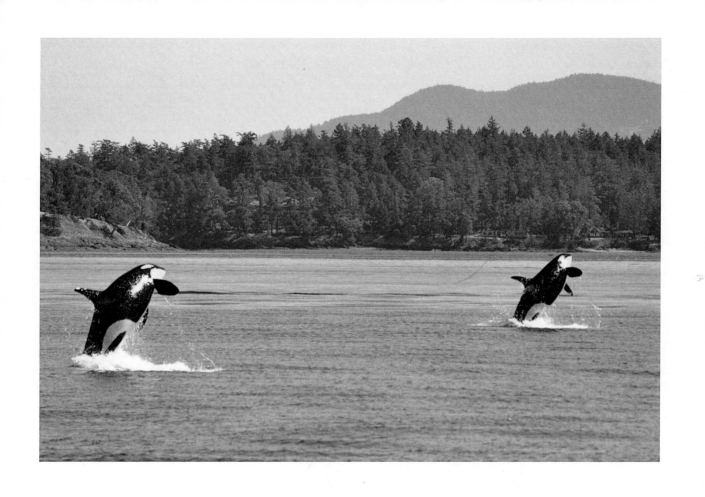

We watch two whales.

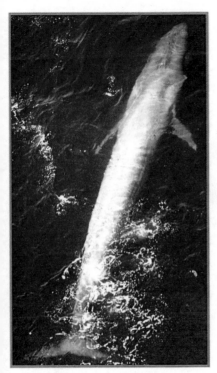

Blue whale

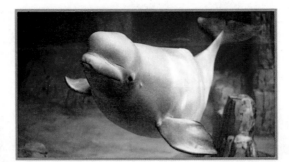

Beluga whale

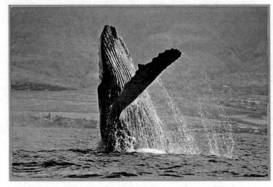

Humpback whale

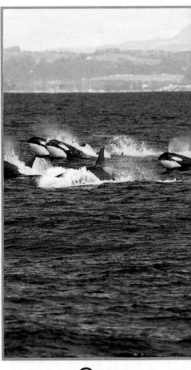

Orca

We watch whales!